ISBN: 978-0-9981964-0-4
First edition, 2016

Author:	Susan Pound
Art:	Edwin Shelton
Cover & Book Layout:	Susan Pound & Edwin Shelton
Digital design:	Jamila Blue

"A great nation is one in which justice, equality, and dignity prevails for all."
Senator Bernie Sanders

THIS BOOK BELONGS TO:

A BERNING FORCE FOR GOOD

REVOLUTION ROAD

A Bernie Bedtime Story

Susan Pound

Art by Edwin Shelton

WWW.ABERNIEBEDTIMESTORY.COM

Listen, my children, and you shall learn

Of the man who inspired us to feel the Bern.

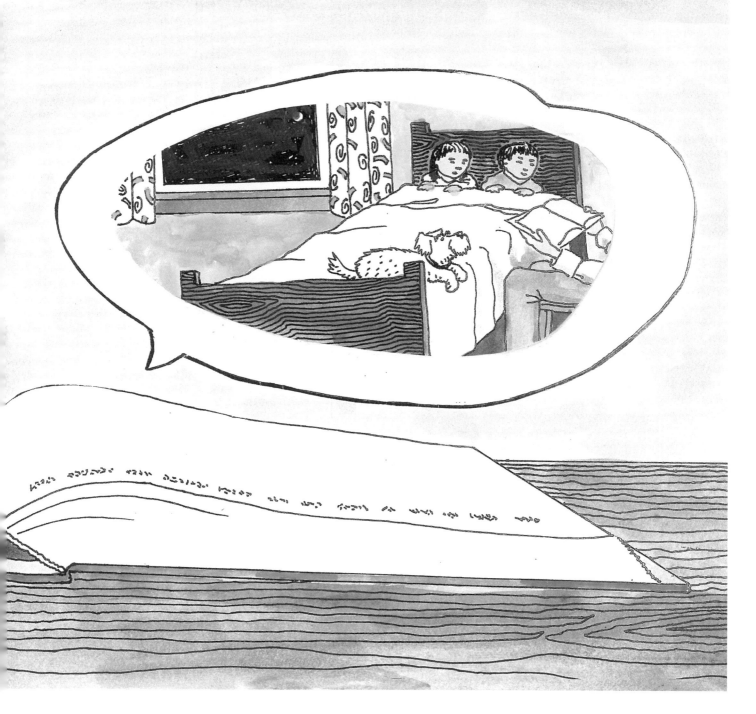

The American Dream needed rescuing,
When Bernie got the call
From our famous Lady Liberty,
The fairest of them all.

Revolution Road

The Revolution keeps on growing.
Truth and justice keep us going.

We'll keep the vision in our sight
There's equality to be won.
The Bern keeps spirits high and bright
Who knew this could be fun?

We'll keep baking till the dish is done
Then all of us will dine
On a Pie that feeds the ninety-nine
As deliciously as the one.

The faster we turn the fiscal key

The trade agreements of the past
Are quite enough to frighten.

Our future shouldn't smell like a deal
Made in a smoke-filled room.

We'll plant a campaign garden
Filled with sweet perfume.

In every town across the land
Change will be selected,

As progressives come to vote in droves
And Berners are elected.

A toast to the Knight with the sword of light
And the courage to fight a Bernie-ish fight.

I wish I may, I wish I might,
Feel the Bern again tonight.

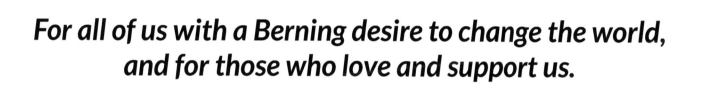

*For all of us with a Berning desire to change the world,
and for those who love and support us.*

ACKNOWLEDGEMENTS

Thank you, Bernie Sanders, for being who you are. Deepest thanks to Berners David Nott and Elisabeth Priller for embodying the inspiration for this book. And for your daily assistance, feedback and research.

Mike Pound (love you, Mikey!) and Laurel Izard, your support, encouragement and patience made the Bernie Journey possible.

To my good friend and magnificent illustrator Edwin Shelton, undying thanks for traveling Revolution Road with me, and breathing its words into living art.

Thank you to Jamila Blue for diving in with digital design, and being an integral team player in moving the book from concept to publication readiness. Eric Van Der Hope, your generous and expert assistance in navigating the publication highway made the journey brighter. Special thanks to our very first book fan, Julie Erwin, and our early cheerleaders—author Stephanie Medlock and publisher Amanda Freymann.

Thanks to: Athena Tainio for reviewing various manuscript drafts, and for one particular line edit suggestion that made a world of difference; Lynn Andrews and my Writing Spirit group for setting the stage for miracles to happen; and Suzy Vance for opening discussions that needed to happen.

John Perkins, thanks as always for your encouragement. And for showing me long ago that things don't get changed by "them"; it's just us doing what we can.

Of course, it takes a Bernie Village. My gratitude goes out to everyone who contributed their valuable time, expertise and support on this literary adventure. Cheers to T.J. Kanczuzewski, Paul Clements, Connor Farrell, Peg Ascherman, Tanis Pound and the folks at Lakeshore Coffee (where the book was born) and Office Max in Michigan City.

Author and illustrator at Lakeshore Coffee 'office'
Photo by Julie Erwin 2016

CPSIA information can be obtained at www.ICGtesting.com
Printed in the USA
LVIW01n0231201216
518050LV00007B/59